contents

christmas at home

101 GINGERBREAD RECIPES AND TRADITIONS

by Mary Herron
with Ellyn Sanna

BARBOUR
PUBLISHING, INC.
Uhrichsville, Ohio

Printed in Canada

© 2001 by Barbour Publishing, Inc.

ISBN 1-58660-257-8

Published by Barbour Publishing, Inc., P.O. Box 719, Uhrichsville, Ohio 44683
http://www.barbourbooks.com

Member of the
Evangelical Christian
Publishers Association

Printed in Canada.

1

The History of Gingerbread

Awake, glad heart! Get up and sing;
It is the birthday of thy King.
HENRY VAUGHAN

What better way to celebrate the King's birthday than with the sweet, fragrant tradition of gingerbread, a tradition that's centuries old?

A Spice for the Rich

The original word for gingerbread came from a Sanskrit word, *singabera*, meaning "root shaped like a horn." Ginger has been grown in India and southern China for countless centuries. The ancient Chinese used it as a medicine.

Ginger was among the first Oriental spices to make their way to Alexandria, and from that great harbor city to Greece and Rome. For many years, though, only the rich used ginger.

An Ancient Treat

Gingerbread is an ancient treat. Egyptians were eating gingerbread when the great pyramid of Cheops was still young—but the first recipe came from Greece, where, in about 2400 B.C., a baker from the island of Rhodes created it. The unleavened, honey-sweetened cakes became famous.

Many things used by the Greeks were eventually copied by the Romans, and this was true of gingerbread. The Romans used ginger to flavor their foods, and they taxed it heavily. Roman legions carried gingerbread recipes to all parts of their vast empire.

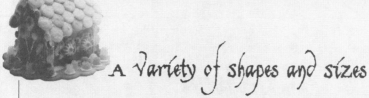

A Variety of shapes and sizes

Gingerbread spread throughout western Europe at the end of the eleventh century; it may have been introduced by the crusaders when they returned from the eastern Mediterranean.

Gingerbread's form varied from location to location. In some places, gingerbread was a soft cake, while in others, it was a crisp, flat cookie; in still other places, the treat came as warm, thick squares of "bread," sometimes served with a pitcher of lemon sauce or cream. Gingerbread was sometimes light and sometimes dark, sometimes sweet and sometimes spicy. Almost always it was cut into shapes—men, women, stars, or animals—and colorfully decorated or dusted with sugar.

Gingerbread "Honours"

By the fifteenth century, ginger and gingerbread were well known in England. Ginger was the second most highly traded spice after pepper in medieval times. Throughout the sixteenth, seventeenth, and eighteenth centuries gingerbread grew more and more fancy. Queen Elizabeth I hired a special artist-baker, whose only job was to create gingerbread lords and ladies in the images of her guests and courtiers to amuse and flatter them. Gingerbread "honours" were popular in other parts of Europe, too. When Peter the Great of Russia was born, his father's friends sent him dozens of huge gingerbread creations. One of the largest was the coat of arms of Moscow, complete with the Kremlin's turrets.

Fairground Gingerbread

Gingerbread also became a fairground treat. Many fairs became known as "gingerbread fairs," and in England gingerbread was called "fairings"—a gift brought from a fair. Certain gingerbread shapes were connected with different seasons: buttons and flowers were common at Easter fairs, and animals and birds were popular at harvest fairs.

If a fair honored a town's patron saint, the saint's image might be stamped into the gingerbread. If the fair was on a special market day, the cakes would be decorated with icing to look like men, animals, valentine hearts, or flowers. Sometimes the dough was simply cut into round "snaps." One English tradition was that unmarried women had to eat gingerbread "husbands" at the fair if they wanted to meet a real husband.

German Gingerbread

Germany has a long tradition of producing flat, shaped gingerbreads. Fourteenth-century Germans formed gingerbread guilds and used carved molds to create gingerbread masterpieces for the aristocracy. German bakers in the 1600s were the first to add molasses to their recipes—and they were the ones who began the tradition of celebrating the holidays with gingerbread.

Every autumn fair in Germany sold gingerbread hearts, decorated with white and colored icing and tied with ribbons. In the city of Nuremberg, gingerbread was not baked in the home but was made exclusively by a guild of master bakers. Nuremberg became known as the "gingerbread capital" of the world, and many gingerbread craftsmen were attracted to the town. Sculptors, painters, woodcarvers, and goldsmiths all contributed to the most beautiful gingerbread cakes in Europe. They carved wooden molds and decorated the gingerbread with frosting or gold paint. Intricate hearts, angels, and wreaths were sold at fairs, carnivals, and markets.

Hansel and Gretel

When the Grimm brothers collected volumes of German fairy tales, they found one about Hansel and Gretel, two children who, abandoned in the woods by destitute parents, discovered a house made of gingerbread and candies. "Nibble, nibble like a mouse," cackled the witch. "Who's that nibbling on my house?"

North American Gingerbread

Gingerbread came to North America from all parts of northern Europe with the settlers who brought with them the traditions of their families. American recipes usually called for fewer spices than their European counterparts; they often made use of ingredients that were only available regionally. For instance, maple syrup gingerbreads were made in New England, while in the South sorghum molasses was used.

In the 1700s, gingerbread "hornbooks" were used to teach children their letters. Hornbooks were in every classroom for hundreds of years. They consisted of flat boards with handles, with a sheet of paper pasted on each board; the paper held a simple lesson for a beginning student and

was protected with a thin sheet of horn. The gingerbread version of this teaching device allowed students to eat each letter of the alphabet as they learned it. What a wonderful way to reinforce learning!

America also linked gingerbread with Christmas. Gingerbread houses were particularly popular in the nineteenth century—elaborate Victorian houses, heavy with candies and sugar icicles.

2
Easiest-ever Gingerbread House

Had I but a penny in the world, thou shouldst have it for gingerbread.
WILLIAM SHAKESPEARE

Few of us have time during the holidays for making the elaborate gingerbread creations our ancestors made. And spending time with family and friends is far more important than impressing them with fancy concoctions. But here's the easiest gingerbread house recipe I could find, sure to delight young and old alike.

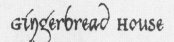

Gingerbread House

5 c. all-purpose flour
2 tsp. ground cinnamon
2 tsp. ground ginger
½ tsp. ground cloves
½ tsp. baking soda

½ tsp. salt
1 c. vegetable shortening
1 c. molasses
2 eggs
Icing (recipe follows)

Preheat oven to 350°F. Using cardboard or waxed paper, cut 1 pattern for each of the 4 walls. In a large bowl, combine flour, cinnamon, ginger, cloves, baking soda, and salt; mix well. In another large bowl, beat shortening and sugar until creamy. Add molasses and eggs; beat until well combined. Slowly stir in the flour mixture until a smooth dough forms. Divide the dough into 3 balls. Place 1 ball of dough on the back of a rimmed cookie sheet. Using a lightly floured rolling pin, roll out the dough to a ⅛-inch thickness. Using the patterns and a sharp knife, cut out the front and back pieces; remove scraps from around the pieces and set aside. Bake pieces 10 to 12 minutes, or until lightly browned around the edges. Allow to cool slightly, then transfer to wire racks to cool completely.

Repeat with another dough ball, cutting and baking the 2 side pieces. Repeat with the third dough ball, cutting and baking the 2 roof pieces. Form the scraps into a ball, roll out, and cut and bake the base piece.

Assemble the house, using the icing as glue, following the directions that follow.

DECORATIONS

mini frosted shredded wheat cereal squares
graham crackers
gumdrops
peppermint sticks
red licorice laces

mini candy-coated
chocolate pieces
red and green mints
spearmint leaves
jelly rings

See instructions on next page.

TO DECORATE:

The roof shingles are mini frosted shredded wheat cereal squares: Cover the roof with icing and attach the squares, frosted side up, in rows, overlapping them slightly. Make the chimney, windows, and doors out of graham crackers and secure them to the house with icing. Pipe icing icicles along the edge of the roof. Make bushes and wreaths from gumdrops—use spearmint leaves for the big bushes and jelly rings with mini candy-coated chocolate ornaments for the wreaths. Frame the windows and doors with peppermint sticks, licorice laces, and candy-coated chocolate pieces. Line mints along the top of the roof.

TO MAKE A SNOWY EXTERIOR:

For snow trees, place an ice-cream cone upside down. With icing in a pastry bag or resealable plastic bag, pipe slightly overlapping rows of zigzags around the cone, starting from the bottom and ending at the top.

For a snowy landscape, sprinkle granulated sugar around the house and make footprints leading up to the door by making small indentations with the blunt end of a pencil or pen.

TO ASSEMBLE THE HOUSE:
Place the base, flat side down, in the center of a large platter or piece of foil-wrapped cardboard. Lay the sides and front and back of the gingerbread house, flat side down, around the base. With the icing in a pastry bag or resealable plastic bag, pipe icing around the edges of each piece.

Carefully lift and press the edges of the back piece and one side piece together, sealing with the icing. Lift the front piece and the remaining side piece and hold in place until the house is secure; let stand for a few minutes. Add additional icing to strengthen the joints.

Place one roof piece in place. Pipe icing along the top inside edge of that piece and place the second roof piece in place. Pipe icing along all

the seams of the house for extra support. Allow icing to dry and set at least 1 hour, preferably overnight, before decorating.

ICING:
3½ c. confectioners' sugar
3 egg whites (If you plan to eat the house, use powdered egg whites for safety's sake.)

In a large bowl, beat confectioners' sugar and egg whites until smooth. Place in a pastry bag fitted with a small tip or in a large resealable plastic bag with a small piece cut off a bottom corner.

3

ginger cookies

Run, run, as fast you can,
but you can't catch me, I'm the gingerbread man.
TRADITIONAL CHILDREN'S STORY

Most of us grew up hearing the story of the mischievous gingerbread man who runs away from his creator. Aren't we all a little like that sugary man? We, too, are always running away from our creator—but Christmas is a good time to stop running. Like the prodigal son, when we turn around, we'll find our Father is waiting with outstretched arms to celebrate our homecoming.

I've included two different recipes for gingerbread people in this section. Try them both and see which one is your favorite!

Stained-Glass Gingerbread Houses

½ c. butter, room temperature

¾ c. granulated sugar

¼ c. dark molasses

1 tbsp. pumpkin-pie spice

2 tsp. ginger

½ tsp baking soda

1 egg

2 tsp. vanilla extract

½ tsp. salt

3 c. all-purpose flour

In a large bowl, with an electric mixer on medium speed, beat butter until creamy. Add sugar, then beat in egg, molasses, pumpkin-pie spice, ginger, vanilla, salt, and soda. Preheat oven to 350°F. Lightly grease baking sheets. Roll out each piece of dough ¼–⅛ inch thick. Cut out cookies with house-shaped cutters. Cut out windows with smaller star- and triangle-shaped cutters. (If dough becomes too soft, refrigerate until firm.) Place cookies on well-greased baking sheets and fill window holes with different colored crushed hard candies. Bake 8 to 12 minutes. Cool on sheets until candy in windows has set; transfer to wire rack and cool completely. Outline the houses and windows with white decorating gel.

Christmas Gingersnaps

2¾ c. flour
1 tbsp. cinnamon
1½ tsp. cloves
1 tsp. each ginger and
   baking soda
⅔ c. butter or margarine,
   softened
¾ c. packed light brown sugar

3 tbsp. each water
   and light molasses
1 tsp. lemon extract
Ornamental Frosting
   (recipe follows)
cinnamon candies and silver
   edible balls

Mix flour, spices, and baking soda; set aside. Cream butter and sugar until light and fluffy. Beat in water, molasses, and lemon extract. Gradually stir in flour mixture until blended. Cover; chill overnight. Roll ¼ dough at a time to ⅛-inch thickness. Using 2-inch cookie cutters, cut in desired shapes. Place ½ inch apart on greased cookie sheets. Bake in preheated 350°F oven 8 minutes or until light brown and crisp. Cool on sheets on rack. Decorate as desired with ornamental frosting, placing candies and silver balls before frosting hardens.

ORNAMENTAL FROSTING:

In a small bowl at high speed beat 1 egg white with ¼ tsp. cream of tartar until frothy. Gradually beat in 1¼ c. confectioners' sugar until thick and glossy.

christmas spice cookies

¾ c. sugar
⅔ c. butter or margarine, softened
¼ c. orange juice
½ c. dark corn syrup
½ c. dark molasses
4½ c. all-purpose flour
¾ c. whole wheat flour

2 tsp. ground ginger
1 tsp. baking soda
1 tsp. salt
½ tsp. ground cloves
½ tsp. ground nutmeg
½ tsp. ground allspice

In a mixing bowl, cream sugar and butter. Blend in orange juice, corn syrup, and molasses. Combine flours, ginger, baking soda, salt, cloves, nutmeg, and allspice. Add to creamed mixture; mix well. Chill 3–4 hours or overnight. Roll a portion of the dough on a lightly floured surface to ¼-inch thickness. Cut into desired shapes. Place 2 inches apart on greased baking sheets. Repeat with remaining dough. Bake at 350°F for 12–14 minutes. Cookies will be soft and chewy if baked 12 minutes—crunchy if baked longer.

Gingerbread Boys

1 c. shortening
1 c. sugar
½ tsp. salt
1 egg
1 tbsp. ginger
1 c. molasses

2 tbsp. vinegar
5 c. sifted enriched flour
1½ tsp. soda
1 tsp. cinnamon
1 tsp. ground cloves

Thoroughly cream shortening, sugar, and salt. Stir in egg, molasses, and vinegar; beat well. Sift together dry ingredients; stir into molasses mixture. Chill (about 3 hours).

On lightly floured surface, roll to ⅛-inch thick. Cut with gingerbread-boy cutter (or draw your own pattern). Place 1 inch apart on greased cookie sheet. Use red cinnamon candies for faces and buttons. Bake in 375°F oven about 6 minutes. Cool slightly; remove from cookie sheet. When thoroughly cool, use confectioners' sugar frosting to pipe on trims. To make cookies stand up, fasten each on skewer with cellophane tape and stick end into plump red apple.

Granny's Ginger Cookies

1 c. butter or margarine, softened
1½ c. sugar
1 egg, lightly beaten
2 tbsp. light corn syrup
2 tbsp. grated orange peel
1 tbsp. cold water
3¼ c. all-purpose flour

2 tsp. baking soda
2 tsp. ground cinnamon
1 tsp. ground ginger
½ tsp. ground cloves
cinnamon candies,
    nonpareils, and/or sprinkles

In a mixing bowl, cream butter and sugar. Add egg, corn syrup, orange peel, and cold water. Combine flour, baking soda, cinnamon, ginger, and cloves; add to creamed mixture and mix well. Chill for at least 1 hour. On a lightly floured surface, roll dough, a portion at a time, to ⅛-inch thickness. Cut into desired shapes. Place on greased baking sheets. Decorate as desired. Bake at 375°F for 6–8 minutes or until lightly browned.

ginger crisps

½ c. butter or margarine
½ c. light molasses
½ c. sugar
1 tbsp. vinegar

2 c. all-purpose flour
1 tsp. cinnamon
½ tsp. ginger
1½ tsp. soda

Grease baking sheets. Start oven 10 minutes before baking; set at 375°F. Measure first 4 ingredients into 1-quart saucepan. Stir well and place over moderate heat and boil gently exactly 3 minutes, stirring constantly. Remove from heat and cool. Meanwhile sift flour, measure, resift 3 times with rest of ingredients. Add dry ingredients to cooled molasses mixture in 2 or 3 portions, mixing until smooth after each. Shape dough into a ball; wrap in waxed paper and chill overnight or for several hours. Roll out thin—about ¹⁄₁₆-inch on a lightly floured pastry cloth with stockinet-covered rolling pin. Cut with a 2-inch round cutter. Place 1½ inches apart on prepared baking sheet. Bake about 7 minutes or until a rich brown. Immediately remove from pan to cake rack to cool.

ginger cream cookies

(for soft, cakelike cookies)

½ c. shortening
1 c. sugar
1 egg
1 c. molasses

4 c. flour
½ tsp. salt
2 tsp. ginger
1 tsp. nutmeg

1 tsp. cloves
1 tsp. cinnamon
1 c. hot water
2 tsp. baking soda

Cream shortening and sugar; blend in egg and molasses. Sift together dry ingredients and add alternately with hot water. Drop by teaspoonfuls and bake in a 400°F oven for about 8 minutes. While still slightly warm, cover with icing.

ICING:
Mix 2 c. confectioners' sugar, 1 tbsp. melted butter, 3 to 4 tbsp. cream, and 1 tsp. vanilla.

old-fashioned molasses cookies

(no sugar or eggs)

8 c. flour
4 tsp. baking soda
½ tsp. salt
1 tbsp. ginger
1 tsp. cinnamon

1 c. lard, melted
3 c. molasses
½ c. butter
10 tbsp. boiling water

Sift dry ingredients. Combine molasses, melted shortening, and boiling water. To this, add 4 cups dry ingredients, and blend well. Add remaining dry ingredients. Chill 1 hour. Roll and cut. Bake at 425°F for 15 minutes.

Three Ginger Cookies

1 stick softened unsalted butter
½ c. dark brown sugar (packed)
1 tbsp. fresh ginger, peeled and
    minced into small pieces
½ tsp. vanilla
1 tbsp. ground ginger

1¼ c. flour
¼ tsp. baking soda
pinch of salt
3–4 pieces crystallized ginger,
    cut into small pieces

Cream the sugar, butter, and fresh ginger until smooth. Add vanilla, and then mix ginger, flour, baking soda, and salt together. Add dry ingredients to butter mixture. Form dough into log about 2 inches square. Wrap in plastic and chill until firm (about 1 hour). Slice log in ¼-inch slices and press a sliver of crystallized ginger into the center of each slice. Bake at 350°F 8 to 10 minutes, until light gold.

century Ginger snaps

(an old-fashioned recipe)

Boil a cup of molasses, add a piece of shortening the size of an egg, a pinch of salt, ⅔ tsp. of soda, and a tsp. of ginger. Cool; add enough flour to roll very thin, and bake in a 400°F oven till done.

Gingerbread Men

2¾ c. all-purpose flour
½ tsp. soda
1 tsp. ginger
½ tsp. cinnamon
½ tsp. salt
½ c. shortening
¼ c. moist brown sugar, packed

¾ c. light
  molasses
1 egg, beaten
½ tsp. grated lemon rind,
  packed
1 tsp. hot water
1 tsp. vinegar

Grease baking sheets lightly, then sprinkle with flour, then tilt and tap lightly to coat with thin film. Start oven 10 minutes before baking; set at 350°F. Sift flour, measure, resift 4 times with next 4 ingredients. With rotary beater, cream shortening until shiny; add moist sugar in 2 or 3 portions, and cream well. Now beat in molasses and egg until fluffy. Clean

off beater, remove; use wooden spoon. Add flour in 2 or 3 portions, mixing until smooth after each, then stir in lemon rind, water, and vinegar until well blended. Cover dough and chill until firm. Divide into 4 portions. Remove 1 portion at a time from refrigerator and roll out ¼-inch thick on a lightly floured pastry cloth. Use snowman or Santa Claus cutter, or make a cardboard pattern to lay on dough and trace around with knife to cut out cookies. Use pancake turner to lift cutouts from pastry cloth and a spatula to carefully slide onto prepared baking sheet. Bend arms and legs to give action poses such as running, etc. Bake about 20 minutes or until nicely browned. Remove from pan immediately to cake racks to cool. Decorate cookies with Confectioners' Icing or Butter Frosting making hair, beard, fur on coat, and stockings. Use currants, candies, and pieces of candied cherries to make eyes, nose, mouth, buttons, etc. Store in metal box with tight-fitting cover 1-layer deep.

swedish ginger cookies

1 c. butter or margarine
1½ c. sugar
1 egg
1½ tbsp. grated orange peel
2 tbsp. dark corn syrup
1 tbsp. water

3¼ c. sifted
    enriched flour
2 tsp. soda
2 tsp. cinnamon
1 tsp. ginger
½ tsp. cloves
blanched almonds

Thoroughly cream the butter and sugar. Add egg and beat till light and fluffy. Add orange peel, corn syrup, and water; mix well. Sift together dry ingredients; stir into creamed mixture. Chill dough thoroughly.

On lightly floured surface, roll to ⅛-inch. (For a sparkly look, sprinkle rolled dough with sugar, then press it in lightly with a rolling pin.) Cut in desired shapes with floured cookie cutter. Place 1 inch apart on ungreased baking sheet. Top each cookie with blanched almond half. Bake in 375°F oven 8 to 10 minutes. Cool on rack.

soft molasses ginger cookies

2¼ c. flour
1 tsp. ginger
1 tsp. cinnamon
¼ tsp. salt
2 tsp. baking soda
2 tbsp. hot water

½ c. shortening
½ c. sugar
½ c. molasses
1 egg
6 tbsp. cold coffee

Heat oven to 400°F. Sift together first four ingredients. Dissolve soda in hot water; stir well. Cool. Work shortening with spoon until fluffy; gradually add sugar and molasses, continuing to cream. Stir in egg; beat well. Add flour mixture alternately with coffee; stir in cooled soda and water. Drop by tablespoonfuls on greased cookie sheet. Bake for 12 minutes or until brown.

Banana-Ginger Cookies

2 c. unsifted all-purpose flour
¾ tsp. salt
¼ tsp. baking soda
¾ c. (1½ sticks) unsalted butter,
    room temperature
1 c. packed light brown sugar

1 c. mashed ripe banana
    (2 medium-sized)
2 tbsp. grated fresh ginger
1 tsp. vanilla
Lemon Glaze
grated lemon rind

Heat oven to 375°F. Coat baking sheet with cooking spray. Mix flour, salt, and soda in bowl. Beat butter and brown sugar in large bowl until smooth and creamy. Beat in banana, ginger, and vanilla. Gradually beat in flour mixture. Drop mixture by rounded tablespoons about 2 inches apart onto prepared baking sheet. Bake in 375°F oven 8 to 10 minutes or until lightly browned and soft-firm to touch. Let stand on sheet on rack 1 to 2 minutes. Remove cookies to racks to cool completely. When cookies are completely cooled, frost with Lemon Glaze and sprinkle with lemon rind.

LEMON GLAZE:
Whisk 2 c. confectioners' sugar, 2 tbsp. milk, 2 tsp. grated lemon rind, $1\frac{1}{2}$ tsp. lemon juice, and $\frac{1}{8}$ tsp. salt in bowl until well blended. If too thick, stir in milk, drop by drop.

Spicy Molasses Cookies

2¼ c. flour
1½ tsp. baking soda
1 tsp. baking powder
1 tsp. ground cinnamon
½ tsp. ground nutmeg
¼ tsp. ground allspice
¼ tsp. salt

½ c. (1 stick) butter,
   at room temp.
¾ c. packed dark-brown sugar
¾ c. dark molasses
1 egg
⅓ c. milk
decorative sugar

Heat oven to 375°F. Coat baking sheet with cooking spray. Combine flour, baking soda, baking powder, cinnamon, nutmeg, allspice, and salt in small bowl. Beat butter, brown sugar in bowl until smooth and creamy. Beat in molasses and egg. Alternately beat in flour mixture and milk, beginning and ending with flour mixture. Drop dough by rounded tablespoons 2 inches apart onto prepared baking sheet. Bake in a 375°F oven 8 to 10 minutes, until soft-firm to touch. Transfer sheet to rack for 1 to 2 minutes. Remove cookies to racks. Sprinkle with sugar. Cool completely.

Gunning Gingerbread Cookies

Our ancestors packed this gingerbread to take with them on hunting trips, and sailors like it because of its long-keeping quality. The original recipe was baked in sheets; the following is baked as a drop cookie.

1 tsp. salt
1 tsp. soda
1½ tsp. ground ginger
½ c. shortening
⅔ c. sugar

1 c. unsulphured molasses
1 tbsp. cider vinegar
3 tbsp. water
3 c. sifted all-purpose flour

Mix together the first 4 ingredients. Gradually add sugar and molasses. Combine vinegar and water and add to the mixture alternately with flour. Drop dough from a tablespoon, 2 inches apart, onto lightly greased cookie sheets. Bake at 350°F for 8 to 10 minutes.

Ginger Puffs

1 c. molasses
1 c. sugar
1 c. melted shortening
1 c. hot water with 2 tsp. soda,
    dissolved

1 tsp. ginger
1 tsp. cinnamon
1 egg
½ tsp. salt
4 heaping c. flour

Beat together first three ingredients. In a separate bowl sift together dry ingredients and add alternately to first mixture with water and soda. Drop by spoonfuls on cookie sheet and bake at 350°F for 8 to 10 minutes.

Mom's Molasses-Ginger Cookies

1 c. lard or other shortening
1 c. sugar
1 c. molasses
2 eggs
2½ tsp. soda, dissolved in
    1½ c. cold coffee

1 tsp. salt
1 tsp. cinnamon
1 tsp. cloves
1 tsp. ginger

Mix together above ingredients and add enough flour to make a soft dough. May be dropped or rolled in balls. Bake at 350°F for 8 to 10 minutes.

Ginger~Snappers

2½ c. all-purpose flour
1 tbsp. plus 2 tsp. ground ginger
2 tsp. ground cinnamon
2 tsp. baking soda
½ tsp. salt
1½ sticks unsalted butter, softened
1 c. firmly packed dark brown sugar

1 large egg,
   at room temp.
¼ c. molasses
1 tbsp. grated lemon peel
¼ c. granulated sugar
26 whole unblanched
   (natural) almonds

Mix flour, ginger, cinnamon, baking soda, and salt in a small bowl. Beat butter and brown sugar in a medium bowl with electric mixer on medium-high speed about 2 minutes until pale and fluffy, scraping bowl twice with a spatula. Beat in egg, then molasses and lemon peel until blended. On low speed, add half the flour mixture, beating just until blended, then beat in remaining half. Roll rounded tablespoonfuls of dough and place on cookie sheet. Press an almond in the center of each cookie. Place on lightly greased cookie sheets and bake at 350°F for 10 to 12 minutes.

3-Way Ginger Cookies

2 c. all-purpose flour
¼ tsp. salt
1 tsp. soda
1 tsp. ginger
½ c. soft butter or half shortening

1 c. sugar
1 egg
¼ c. dark molasses
1 tbsp. vinegar

Grease baking sheets lightly. Preheat oven to 375°F for 10 minutes before baking. Sift flour, measure, resift 4 times with next 3 ingredients. Cream butter until shiny, add sugar gradually and cream well. Beat in egg until fluffy. Stir in molasses, then vinegar. Add flour in 2 portions, mixing until smooth after each portion.

1ST WAY
Drop by level dessertspoonfuls onto waxed paper; shape into balls, rolling lightly between buttered palms of hands. Arrange on prepared sheets. Bake 12 to 13 minutes or until delicately browned. Let stand on sheet 1 minute, then remove to cake racks to cool.

2ND WAY
After shaping dough into balls, dip into ½ c. chopped nuts spread on waxed paper. Place on baking sheet, nut-side up, and bake as above.

3RD WAY
Shape balls as above. Dip into a mixture of 3 tbsp. granulated sugar and 1 tbsp. grated orange rind. Place on baking sheet, sugar-side up. Bake as above.

Ginger~Marmalade Thumbprints

2 tbsp. ginger marmalade
2 tbsp. chopped green or
    red candied cherries
1 tbsp. finely chopped pecans
2½ c. flour
½ tsp. ground nutmeg

½ tsp. salt
1 c. (2 sticks) butter, softened
⅔ c. sugar
1 large egg
2 tsp. vanilla extract

Heat oven to 375°F. In small bowl, combine marmalade, cherries, and pecans; set aside. In medium-sized bowl, combine flour, nutmeg, and salt; set aside.

In large bowl, with electric mixer on medium speed, beat butter and sugar until light and fluffy. Beat in egg and vanilla. Reduce mixer speed to low; gradually beat in flour mixture until well mixed.

Measure a scant tbsp. of dough and shape into a ball. Repeat process with remaining dough to make a total of 36 balls. Place balls 2 inches apart on ungreased large baking sheet. With thumb, make an indentation in top of each ball of dough. Spoon about ¼ tsp. marmalade mixture into each indentation. Bake 10 to 12 minutes until edges are lightly browned. Cool cookies 2 minutes on baking sheets, then transfer to wire racks and cool completely. Store in airtight container.

Bran Gingersnaps

1¼ c. flour
1½ tsp. ginger
¼ tsp. baking soda
¼ tsp. salt

⅓ c. butter or other shortening
½ c. molasses
¼ c. firmly packed brown sugar
1½ c. bran flakes or raisin bran

Mix flour with ginger, soda, and salt. Combine butter, molasses, and brown sugar in saucepan; heat until butter is melted, stirring constantly. Remove from heat. Add cereal and mix well. Add flour mixture; mix thoroughly. Chill until firm. Roll ⅛-inch thick on lightly floured board. Cut with 2½-inch cookie cutter. Place on greased baking sheets. Bake at 350°F for about 8 to 10 minutes or until just brown around edges.

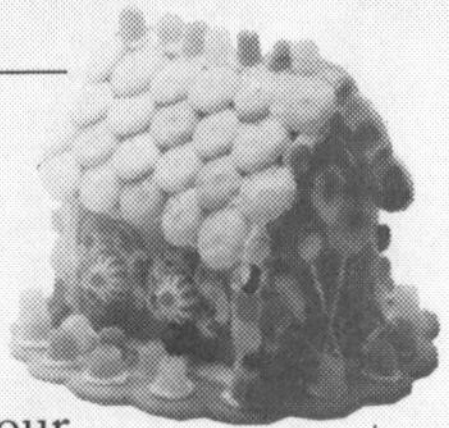

Frosted Ginger Cookies

1½ c. butter or margarine
1 c. sugar
1 c. packed brown sugar
2 eggs
½ c. molasses
2 tsp. vanilla extract

4½ c. all-purpose flour
1 tbsp. ground ginger
2 tsp. baking soda
2 tsp. ground cinnamon
½ tsp. salt
½ tsp. ground cloves

FROSTING:
⅓ c. packed brown sugar
2 c. confectioners' sugar
2 tbsp. butter or margarine
¼ c. milk

½ tsp. vanilla extract or
    caramel flavoring
Pinch salt

In a mixing bowl, cream butter and sugars. Add the eggs, one at a time, beating well after each addition. Stir in molasses and vanilla; mix well. Combine dry ingredients; gradually add to creamed mixture. Drop by tablespoonfuls 2 inches apart onto ungreased baking sheets. Bake at 325°F for 12–15 minutes or until cookies spring back when touched lightly (do not overbake). Remove to wire racks. For frosting, in a medium saucepan, bring sugars and butter to a boil; boil for 1 minute, stirring constantly. Stir in milk; bring to a boil. Remove from the heat (mixture will look curdled at first). Cool for 3 minutes. Add vanilla and salt; mix well. Frost warm cookies.

Ginger Almond Cookies

1½ c. shortening
1½ c. sugar
¾ c. light molasses
4 c. flour
1½ tsp. soda

1½ tsp. salt
1 tbsp. plus 1 tsp. ginger
1 tbsp. cinnamon
1 tbsp. cloves
1½ c. almonds, finely chopped

Cream shortening, sugar, and molasses until fluffy. Measure flour and mix dry ingredients. Stir into creamed mixture. Add almonds. Shape in 2 thick rolls, each 2 inches in diameter. Wrap in waxed paper; refrigerate several hours until very firm. Heat oven to 350°F. Cut in ¼-inch slices. Bake on lightly greased baking sheet 12 to 15 minutes.

Merry christmas Ginger cookies

⅓ c. shortening
⅓ c. sugar
1 egg
⅔ c. honey

1 tsp. lemon flavoring
2¾ c. flour
1 tsp. soda
1 tsp. salt

Mix shortening, sugar, egg, honey, and flavoring thoroughly. Measure and stir together flour, soda, salt; blend in. Chill dough.

Heat oven to 375°F. Roll dough out ½-inch thick. Cut into desired shapes. Place 1 inch apart on lightly greased baking sheet. Bake 8 to 10 minutes, or until no imprint remains when touched lightly. When cool, ice and decorate as desired.

pecan spice cookies

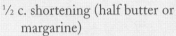

½ c. shortening (half butter or
   margarine)
1¼ c. brown sugar (packed)
1 egg
1¾ c. flour
½ tsp. salt
½ tsp. ginger

½ tsp. cinnamon
½ tsp. cloves
½ tsp. nutmeg
⅓ c. chopped pecans
4 to 5 dozen pecan halves
   (for tops)

Heat oven to 375°F. Mix shortening, sugar, and egg thoroughly. Measure flour and blend dry ingredients; stir into shortening mixture. Stir in chopped pecans. Roll dough in 1 inch balls. Place 2 inches apart on greased baking sheet. Place a pecan half on top of each cookie, flattening slightly. Bake 10 to 12 minutes. For softer cookies, store in tight container with an apple slice.

Moravian Ginger Cookies

This cookie is crisp, spicy, and paper-thin. The Moravians, who founded Bethlehem, Pennsylvania, on Christmas Eve 1741, brought this cookie recipe with them.

⅓ c. molasses
3 tbsp. shortening
2 tbsp. brown sugar
1¼ c. flour
½ tsp. salt

½ tsp. soda
¼ tsp. each cinnamon, ginger, and cloves
dash each nutmeg and allspice

Mix molasses, shortening, and sugar thoroughly. Measure flour and stir together remaining ingredients; blend in. Work with hands until well blended. Cover; chill about 4 hours. (Thorough chilling is needed to make dough hold together.)

Heat oven to 375F°. Roll dough out paper-thin, a little at a time. Cut in desired shapes. Place on greased baking sheet. Bake 5 to 6 minutes or until lightly browned. If desired, when cool, frost with icing.

Ginger Drop Cookies and Easy Ginger Drop Variations

Gradually add ½ c. lukewarm water to a gingerbread mix.
Mix until smooth. Chill. Heat oven to 375°F. Drop dough
by teaspoonfuls on lightly greased baking sheet. Bake 10 to 12 minutes.

VARIATIONS

COCONUT GINGER:
Stir in 1 c. shredded coconut.

CHOCOLATE CHIP GINGER:
Stir in 1 c. semisweet chocolate pieces and ½ c. chopped nuts.

DATE-NUT GINGER:
Stir in ½ c. dates, finely cut, and ½ c. chopped nuts.

FRUIT GINGER:
Stir in 1 c. cut-up candied fruit and ½ c. chopped nuts.

JEWELED GINGER:
Stir in ⅔ c. gumdrops, cut in small pieces, and ½ c. chopped nuts.

PEANUT GINGER:
Stir in 1 c. chopped peanuts.

PEANUT BUTTER GINGER:
Stir in ½ c. peanut butter (creamy or chunk-style), ½ c. brown sugar (packed), and ½ c. chopped salted peanuts with the water.

GINGER CREAMS:
Add 1 c. canned pumpkin. Frost tops with icing.

ginger-oatmeal cookies

1 package gingerbread mix
1 c. applesauce
2 c. quick-cooking rolled oats

½ c. chopped nuts
½ c. chopped raisins,
  if desired

Heat oven to 400°F. Mix all ingredients. Drop dough by teaspoonfuls about 1 inch apart on well-greased baking sheet. Bake 10 to 12 minutes. Frost if desired.

Maple Gingersnaps

1½ c. butter-flavored shortening
1½ c. sugar
1 c. dark-grade maple syrup
2 eggs
4½ c. all-purpose flour

2½ tsp. baking soda
2 tsp. cinnamon
2 tsp. ground cloves
4 tsp. ginger
½ c. sugar plus 1 tbsp. cinnamon for rolling

Cream shortening and sugar. Whisk in the syrup and eggs. Sift together the dry ingredients (except sugar and cinnamon for rolling) and add to the egg mixture. Chill batter well. Roll into balls approximately 1 inch in diameter. Roll balls in mixture of sugar and cinnamon and place 2 inches apart on greased baking sheets. Bake at 350°F for 15 minutes. Remove from oven, let rest for 1 minute, then remove to rack.

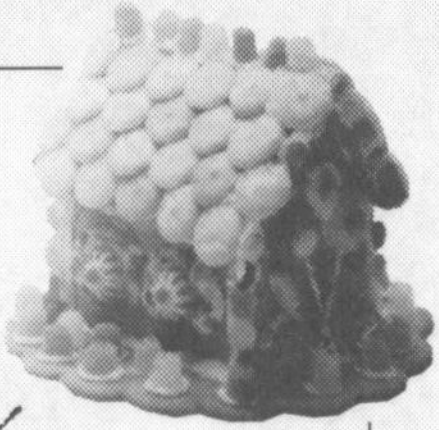

How to Make Perfect Drop Cookies

Mix dough as directed. If dough is soft, chill. Spoon up dough as recipe directs. Push dough onto baking sheet with another spoon, peaking up dough. Bake minimum time in preheated oven. Test cookies by touching center lightly with finger. If almost no imprint remains and cookie is golden brown, it is done. Perfect drop cookies have:

- fairly uniform mound shape
- delicate brown exterior
- good flavor

How to make perfect rolled cookies

Mix dough as directed. Using part of dough and keeping rest chilled, lightly roll dough to desired thickness; the thinner you roll, the crisper the cookies. Rub flour into rolling pin cover and cloth to prevent sticking. To cut: dip cookie cutter in flour, shake off excess, cut with steady pressure. Cut as many cookies from each rolling as possible. Cut diamonds or squares with knife. Carefully lift cutout cookies to baking sheet with spatula. Bake. Perfect rolled cookies have:

- uniform shape of cutter
- light brown surface
- crisp texture or soft texture, depending on thickness
- rich, delicate flavor

How to Make Perfect Molded Cookies

Mix dough as directed. Richer, softer doughs call for chilling before shaping. Roll into balls between palms of hands. Bake as balls or flatten with bottom of glass or by crisscrossing with fork. For attractive crescents, fruits, candy canes, etc., take your time and mold cookies carefully. As you become more skillful, molding will go more quickly. Perfect molded cookies have:

- uniform shape
- delicate brown exterior
- crisp, tender eating quality
- pleasing flavor

How to Make
Perfect Refrigerator Cookies

Mix dough as directed. With hands, shape dough into long, smooth roll of diameter recipe suggests. If desired, add a festive touch by rolling in finely chopped nuts, colored sugar, or chocolate shot. Wrap in waxed paper, twisting ends. Chill in refrigerator until firm enough to slice easily. When ready to bake, slice desired thickness using thin, sharp knife. You can refrigerate three to four days. Perfect refrigerator cookies have:

- uniform, thin slices
- light brown surface
- crisp, crunchy texture
- rich flavor

cookie Baking Hints

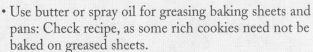

- Use butter or spray oil for greasing baking sheets and pans: Check recipe, as some rich cookies need not be baked on greased sheets.
- Try to make all cookies in a batch the same size to insure uniform baking.
- Bake a test cookie to see if consistency of dough is right. If cookie spreads more than desired, add 1 to 2 more tablespoons of flour. If cookie seems dry or crumbly, add 1 to 2 tablespoons milk to dough.
- If baking 1 sheet of cookies at a time, bake in center of oven. If baking 2 sheets, place oven racks so oven is divided in thirds.
- Look at cookies when minimum baking time is up. Try not to over-bake. Remove from baking sheet to cooling rack with spatula immediately because cookies continue to bake until removed from baking sheet.
- If possible, have a second cool baking sheet ready as cookie dough spreads on a hot baking sheet.

How to store cookies

Store crisp, thin cookies in container with loose cover.
Store soft cookies in container with a tight-fitting cover.

HOW TO FREEZE COOKIES:
Baked cookies and cookie dough may be frozen nine to twelve months.
Pack baked cookies in a rigid box, lining the box and separating each
layer of cookies with transparent plastic wrap. The clinging quality of the
plastic keeps air from reaching and drying out the cookies. Shape refrigerator cookie dough in roll; wrap in foil or transparent plastic wrap. Place
drop or rolled cookie dough in frozen food container or wrap in foil or
transparent plastic wrap.

Helpful Hints for
Sending Cookies in the Mail

What cookies travel best?

Bar cookies, drop cookies, and fruit cookies travel well. Avoid fragile rolled cookies that may crumble before they reach their destination.

What wrapping materials will be needed?

Use a sturdy packing box—heavier than ordinary pasteboard. Line with waxed paper. Have plenty of filler: crushed or shredded newspaper, wrapping paper, tissue paper, unbuttered and unsalted popcorn, or a puffed cereal.

How should cookies be packed?

Wrap each cookie separately in waxed paper or transparent plastic wrap. Or place cookies bottom-to-bottom in pairs and wrap each pair. Then pack cookies in layers. Place a layer of filler in bottom of packing box and cover it with waxed paper. Lay wrapped cookies closely together on waxed paper. Alternate layers of cookies and fill with enough filler over the last layer of cookies to act as padding at the top. The box should be so full that you have to press down the lid to get it on.

Wrap the box and address plainly.

Wrap the box tightly with heavy paper. Address plainly with permanent ink, covering the address with transparent tape. Mark the box PERISHABLE AND FRAGILE. Be sure to use the correct amount of postage.

4
gingerbread cakes

Have you ever heard of the Sugar-Plum Tree?
'Tis a marvel of great renown!
...The fruit that it bears is so wondrously sweet
(As those who have tasted it say)
That good little children have only to eat
Of that fruit to be happy next day.
...And up in that tree sits a chocolate cat,
And a gingerbread dog prowls below....
GEOFFREY SCOTT

We hear so much about the evils of sugar these days. Sometimes (why not at Christmas?) we need to forget about all the shoulds and shouldn'ts—and simply delight in the sweet, magical flavors of Christmas. Like good little children, let us gather round the "Sugar-Plum Tree" and enjoy some of the gingerbread cake recipes I've collected here.

Honey Ginger Cake

2¼ c. cake flour
2 tsp. soda
1 tsp. salt
1 tsp. ginger
1 tsp. cinnamon
½ c. shortening

½ c. brown sugar, packed
1 egg
1 c. honey
1 c. buttermilk
½ pt. whipping cream
walnuts, broken

Line bottoms of two 9-inch layer pans with waxed paper; grease paper and sides of pans. Start oven 10 minutes before baking; set at 350°F. Sift flour, measure, and resift 3 times with next 4 ingredients. Cream shortening, add sieved sugar gradually, and cream thoroughly. With rotary beater, beat in

egg until smooth and fluffy, then add honey until blended. Add flour mixture and milk alternately in 3 or 4 portions, beginning and ending with flour and beating with wooden spoon until blended after each. Turn into prepared pans. Bake about 30 minutes or until cake tests done. Remove to cake racks to cool in pans 5 minutes, then carefully turn out on racks, remove paper, and quickly turn right side up to finish cooling. Whip cream stiff, sweeten with 1 tsp. honey, and spread between layers and over top. Sprinkle with walnuts. Store in refrigerator an hour or two before serving.

Fresh Ginger Cake

1½ c. sifted flour
1 tsp. baking soda
¼ tsp. salt
7 tbsp. vegetable oil
½ c. plus 1 tbsp. apple juice
½ c. brown sugar
¼ c. light molasses

¼ c. dark corn syrup
1 egg
3 tbsp. grated fresh ginger
heavy cream, whipped
  (optional)
candied ginger, finely
  chopped (optional)

Sift together the flour, baking soda, and salt. In a mixing bowl, combine the oil and the apple juice. Beat in the sugar, molasses, and corn syrup. Beat in the egg. Add the grated fresh ginger and the flour mixture, and mix well. Pour the batter into a buttered and floured pan. Bake in a preheated 350°F oven for 30 to 35 minutes, or until the cake is firm to the touch in the center and has pulled away slightly from the sides of the pan. Cool the cake in the pan for five minutes, then turn it out onto a wire rack. Cut the cake into squares and serve it still warm or at room temperature. For special occasions, serve topped with whipped cream and finely chopped candied ginger.

ginger~caramel cupcakes

CARAMEL:

⅓ c. water plus 2 tbsp.   ¾ c. granulated sugar

Place ⅓ c. water near stove. Heat sugar and 2 tbsp. water in small saucepan over medium-high heat until sugar starts to dissolve, 3 to 4 minutes. Swirl pan constantly as mixture starts to turn golden in color. When mixture begins to smoke, turns amber-colored, and sugar is dissolved (1 to 2 minutes) remove from heat. Watch very carefully during last stage, because sugar mixture will turn very quickly. Very carefully add ⅓ c. water in 3 additions to saucepan, holding pan at arm's length, to avoid spattering; mixture is very hot. Stir until caramel is dissolved, returning to heat if needed. Pour into 1-cup glass measuring cup. Add water to equal ¾ cup if needed. Let stand until cooled to room temperature. Use ½ cup for batter and ½ cup for frosting.

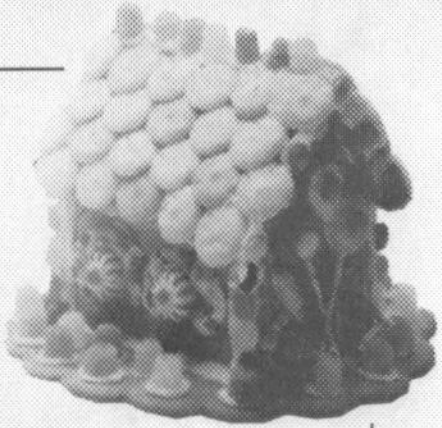

BATTER:

1 c. all-purpose flour	6 tbsp. (¾ stick)
¾ c. tsp. baking powder	unsalted butter,
¼ tsp. baking soda	at room temperature
½ tsp. ground ginger	⅓ c. granulated sugar
¼ tsp. ground cinnamon	1 egg
¼ tsp. salt	⅓ c. sour cream

Heat oven to 350°F. Line sixteen 2½-inch muffin cups with foil liners. Coat lightly with cooking spray.

Stir together flour, baking powder, baking soda, ginger, cinnamon, and salt in small bowl.

Beat butter and sugar in bowl until light and fluffy, 1 minute. Beat in egg and sour cream until blended. Alternately fold in flour mixture and ½ cup cooled caramel mixture in 3 additions, beginning and ending with flour. Spoon into muffin cups. Bake in 350°F oven 25 minutes or until

wooden pick inserted in centers comes out clean. Cool in
pan on rack 5 minutes. Remove cupcakes from pans; cool
completely on wire rack.

FROSTING:
6 tbsp. (¾ stick) unsalted butter, at room temperature
2½ to 3 c. confectioners' sugar, sifted
¼ c. reserved caramel mixture (from step 3)

Beat butter in medium-sized bowl until smooth. Gradually beat in confectioners' sugar and remaining ¼ cup caramel mixture; beat 1 minute or
until creamy. Frost cupcakes. Garnish with currants, grapes, and goose-
berries if desired.

buttermilk gingerbread

1½ c. all-purpose flour or
    1⅔ c. cake flour
¼ tsp. salt
½ tsp. soda
½ tsp. cinnamon
½ tsp. ginger

½ tsp. allspice
½ c. soft butter
½ c. sugar
1 egg
½ c. molasses
½ c. plus 2 tbsp. buttermilk

Line bottom of an 8 x 8 x 2-inch pan with waxed paper—grease paper and sides of pan lightly. Start oven 10 minutes before baking; set at 350°F. Sift flour, measure, resift 3 times with salt, soda, and spices. With rotary beater, cream butter until smooth, add sugar and egg and beat until smooth and fluffy; add molasses and beat vigorously 2 minutes longer. Clean off beater and remove. Add flour mixture and buttermilk alternately in 3 or 4 portions, beginning and ending with flour and beating with wooden spoon until smooth after each. Turn batter into prepared pan. Bake 25 to 30 minutes. Cool in pan on cake rack 4 minutes, then turn out on rack, strip off paper quickly, and invert. Serve warm with whipped cream, apple sauce, or melted marshmallows. If glass baking dish is used, bake at 325°F.

Upside-Down Apple Gingerbread

¼ c. butter or margarine, melted
2 large apples, peeled,
   cored, and sliced

⅓ c. packed
   brown sugar

GINGERBREAD:
½ c. butter or margarine, melted
½ c. molasses
½ c. sugar
⅓ c. packed brown sugar
1 egg
2 c. all-purpose flour
1 tsp. baking soda

1 tsp. ground cinnamon
1 tsp. ground ginger
½ tsp. ground cloves
½ tsp. salt
¼ tsp. ground nutmeg
¾ c. hot tea

Pour butter into a 9-inch square baking pan. Arrange apples over butter; sprinkle with brown sugar and set aside. For gingerbread, combine butter, molasses, sugars, and egg in a mixing bowl; mix well. Combine dry ingredients; add to sugar mixture alternately with hot tea. Mix well; pour over apples. Bake at 350°F for 45–50 minutes or until the cake tests done. Cool for 3–5 minutes. Loosen sides and invert onto a serving plate. Serve warm.

sour cream gingerbread

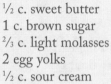

½ c. sweet butter
1 c. brown sugar
⅔ c. light molasses
2 egg yolks
½ c. sour cream
1½ c. sifted flour
1 tsp. ginger

1 tsp. cinnamon
¼ tsp. nutmeg
¼ tsp. cloves
1 tsp. soda
2 tbsp. hot water
2 egg whites, beaten

Cream the butter and sugar until light and smooth. Add the molasses, egg yolks, and sour cream. Sift the flour with the spices and add to the butter mixture. Dissolve the soda in the hot water and add it. Fold in the stiffly beaten egg whites last. Bake in a greased, floured 8 x 11-inch pan at 350°F about 25 to 30 minutes. When it shrinks from the sides of the pan or springs back from the touch of the finger, it is done. This is delicious served hot with butter.

orange gingerbread

½ c. sweet butter
½ c. light brown sugar
½ c. light molasses
1 egg, beaten
juice and grated rind of 1 orange

½ c. cold strong tea
1¾ c. pastry flour
¾ tsp. soda
1 tsp. ginger

Cream the butter and sugar until smooth, then add the molasses, beaten egg, juice, and rind. Beat well; add the tea, and the flour sifted with the soda and ginger. Bake in an 8 x 11-inch pan, which has been greased and floured, 30 minutes at 350°F.

Mame's Gingerbread

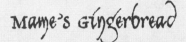

³/₄ c. sweet butter
³/₄ c. brown sugar
³/₄ c. light molasses
2 eggs, beaten
2½ c. sifted flour
1 tsp. cinnamon

1 tsp. ginger
1 tsp. cloves
2 tsp. soda
1 c. boiling water,
    orange juice, or strong
    black coffee

Cream the butter and sugar; when smooth add the molasses. Beat the eggs until light and add them. Sift the flour with the spices and add to the egg mixture. Dissolve the soda in the hot liquid and add it to the batter. Bake in a long shallow greased, floured pan at 350°F about 35 to 40 minutes.

Eggless Gingerbread

1 c. molasses
1 c. sour cream
2 tsp. baking powder
2¼ c. sifted flour

2 tsp. ginger
⅛ tsp. salt
½ c. melted butter

Mix the molasses with the sour cream and baking powder. Sift the flour with the dry ingredients and combine with the sour cream mixture. Add the melted butter last and bake in a shallow 8 x 11-inch greased, floured pan 35 minutes at 350°F.

Hot Water Gingerbread

1 c. all-purpose flour
½ c. sugar
1 tsp. salt
1 tsp. ground ginger
½ tsp. baking soda

1 egg
½ c. molasses
½ c. hot water
1 tbsp. butter or margarine,
   softened

TOPPING:
2 tbsp. sugar   2 tsp. ground cinnamon

Combine flour, sugar, salt, ginger, and baking soda; set aside. In a mixing bowl, beat egg, molasses, water, and butter until smooth. Gradually add the dry ingredients; beat for 1 minute. Pour into a greased 8-inch square baking pan. Combine the sugar and cinnamon; sprinkle evenly over gingerbread. Bake at 350°F for 25 minutes or until a wooden pick inserted near the center comes out clean. Cool completely before cutting. Top each square with whipped topping.

Haddon Hall Gingerbread

2¼ c. all-purpose flour or
   cake flour
⅓ c. sugar
1 c. dark molasses
¾ c. hot water
½ c. shortening

1 egg
1 tsp. soda
1 tsp. ginger
1 tsp. cinnamon
¾ tsp. salt

Heat oven to 325°F. Grease and flour square pan, 9 x 9 x 2 inches. Measure all ingredients into large mixer bowl. Blend ½ minute on low speed, scraping bowl constantly. Beat 3 minutes medium speed, scraping bowl constantly. Pour into pan. Bake 50 minutes or until wooden pick inserted in center comes out clean.

Beat 1 package (8 oz.) cream cheese, softened, and ¼ c. milk until fluffy. Cut gingerbread into 12 pieces. Split each piece to make 2 layers. Fill layers with about ½ tbsp. of the cream cheese mixture. Top pieces with remaining cream cheese mixture. Serve with warm lemon sauce.

Iowa Gingerbread

2 tsp. baking soda
1 c. hot coffee
½ c. softened butter
1 c. molasses
1 tsp. ginger

1 tsp. cinnamon
1 tsp. cloves
2½ c. flour
1 c. raisins
2 eggs, well beaten

Preheat oven to 375°F. In a bowl dissolve baking soda in coffee. Add rest of ingredients and pour into a lightly greased baking pan (13 x 9 inches). Bake for 30 to 40 minutes, until a fork inserted into middle comes out clean.

country gingerbread

1 c. molasses
1 c. sour milk (If you don't have
    sour milk, add 2 tsp. vinegar
    to $\frac{1}{2}$ c. milk.)
$2\frac{1}{4}$ c. sifted flour

$1\frac{3}{4}$ tsp. baking powder
2 tsp. ginger
$\frac{1}{2}$ tsp. salt
1 egg, beaten
$\frac{1}{2}$ c. oil

Mix molasses and milk. Sift dry ingredients together. Add to milk mixture. Add egg and oil. Beat until smooth and creamy. Pour into greased 9 x 9-inch pan. Bake at 350°F about 30 minutes.

Grandmother's Gingerbread

½ c. brown sugar
½ c. solid shortening
2 eggs
¼ c. molasses
1¼ c. sifted flour
¼ tsp. salt

1 tsp. baking soda
¼ tsp. baking powder
1¼ tsp. ginger
1 tsp. cinnamon
¼ tsp. ground cloves
½ c. hot water

In large bowl, combine brown sugar, Crisco, eggs, and molasses; blend well. Combine flour, salt, soda, baking powder, and spices; gradually blend into molasses mixture. Blend in hot water; pour batter into greased and floured 9 x 9 x 2-inch baking pan. Bake at 350°F for 25 to 30 minutes. Serve warm with Citrus Fluff.

See instructions for Citrus Fluff on next page.

CITRUS FLUFF:
In small saucepan, beat 1 egg; add ½ cup sugar, 1 tsp. grated orange peel, 1 tsp. grated lemon peel, and 2 tbsp. lemon juice. Cook and stir over low heat until thickened, about 5 minutes. Cool thoroughly. Fold in 1 cup whipping cream, whipped. Chill. Spoon onto squares of warm gingerbread. Garnish with a twist of orange.

Inverness Gingerbread

12 oz. flour
4 oz. fine oatmeal
8 oz. butter
12 oz. molasses

4 oz. candied
    lemon peel
1 oz. green ginger
½ c. cream or whole milk

Mix the flour and oatmeal together. Cream the butter, and beat in the flour mixture and cream alternately. Stir in the molasses; then add the ginger and peel, cut into fine shreds. Work the whole into a light dough, turn into a well-greased tin, and bake in a moderate oven at 350°F for about 45 minutes.

soft gingerbread

1 c. sugar
1 c. molasses
½ c. butter or other shortening
3 c. flour
1 c. sour milk
2 tsp. ginger

2 tsp. cinnamon
1 tsp. cloves
¼ tsp. nutmeg
2 eggs, well beaten
1 tsp. soda, dissolved in
    ¼ c. boiling water

Cream the shortening and sugar, add the eggs and molasses, and mix well. Sift the flour and spices, and add alternately with the milk to the first mixture. Stir in the dissolved soda. Pour into well-greased cake pan and bake at 350°F for 30 minutes.

Laura Ingalls Wilder's Gingerbread

This recipe comes from a letter written by the well-known author.

1 c. brown sugar blended with ½ c. shortening
½ c. molasses mixed well with above
2 tsp. baking soda in 1 c. of boiling water
  (Be sure cup is full of water after foam runs off into cake batter.)

To 3 c. of flour, add 1 tsp. each of the following spices: ginger, cinnamon, allspice, nutmeg, cloves, and ½ tsp. salt. Sift all into mixture and mix well. Lastly, add 2 well-beaten eggs.

The mixture should be quite thin. Bake in a moderate oven for 30 minutes. A chocolate frosting adds to the goodness.

Edinburgh Gingerbread

8 oz. flour
4 oz. butter
4 oz. molasses
2 oz. sugar
4 oz. raisins
2 oz. almonds

1 tsp. baking soda
1 tsp. cinnamon
1 tsp. cloves
1 tsp. ginger
2 eggs

Sift the flour, soda, and spices into a bowl. Put the butter, sugar, and molasses into a small saucepan and bring to a boil. Beat the eggs, and pour the molasses over them, stirring vigorously. Add this mixture to the dry ingredients and beat thoroughly. Put into a buttered cake-tin and bake for an hour at 350°F.

Marmalade Gingerbread

1 package (14 oz.) gingerbread mix   ½ c. orange marmalade
¾ c. orange juice

Combine gingerbread mix, orange juice, and marmalade; blend according to package directions. Pour into greased 8- or 9-inch square dish. Shield each corner with a triangle of foil; mold foil around dish. Cook over low heat 8 minutes and at medium-high heat 6 to 8 minutes, or until toothpick inserted near center comes out clean. Let stand 10 minutes. Store, covered, until ready to serve.

cream cheese Filling for gingerbread

½ c. dates sliced
½ c. orange marmalade
½ c. stiffly beaten heavy cream

6 oz. cream cheese
⅛ tsp. salt

Beat cheese until soft. Beat in marmalade and salt. Fold in dates and whipped cream. Split the gingerbread, spreading filling between layers and on top. Serve while warm. Sufficient for a 9-inch square pan of gingerbread.

Muster Gingerbread

This is an old recipe, once used to feed the colonial armies.

1½ c. sifted flour
½ tsp. baking powder
½ tsp. salt
¼ c. shortening
½ tsp. soda
½ tsp. ground cinnamon
½ tsp. ground ginger

½ tsp. ground nutmeg
¼ tsp. ground cloves
¼ c. sugar
½ c. molasses
1 large egg
½ c. hot water

Sift together the first 3 ingredients and set aside. Blend shortening with soda and spices. Gradually add sugar and molasses, mixing well. Stir in ½ cup of the flour mixture. Beat in egg. Add remaining flour alternately with hot water. Beat batter ½ minute. Turn batter into a well-greased, lightly floured 9 x 9 x 2-inch pan. Bake in an oven preheated to 350°F for 25 minutes or until toothpick inserted in the center comes out clean. Cool and cut into 12 bars. Store airtight.

5
Other Gingerbread Pastries and Desserts

Nose, nose, nose, nose!
And who gave thee this jolly red nose?
Nugmegs and ginger, cinnamon and cloves,
And they gave me this jolly red nose.
THOMAS RAVENSCROFT, 1592–1635

Spices like ginger stimulate our circulation, bringing the blood to our faces. At Christmastime, enjoy these gingery treats—they may make us look like Santa Claus himself, with his jolly red nose, but that's part of the fun!

Ginger-Pignoli Shortbread

¾ c. confectioners' sugar
⅓ c. crystallized ginger
½ tsp. salt
6 tbsp. pine nuts (pignoli)

2¼ c. all-purpose flour
1 c. (2 sticks) chilled
unsalted butter, cut
into pats

Coat two 9-inch round baking pans with nonstick cooking spray. Combine confectioners' sugar, crystallized ginger, and salt in food processor. Whirl until the ginger is finely chopped, for about 10 seconds. Add the flour and whirl until combined. Add butter and pulse until the butter is finely chopped. Whirl until mixture starts to come together. Crumble mixture into prepared pans, dividing evenly. Press mixture evenly over bottoms of pans; press flat bottom of glass measure on top of dough to compact and level dough. Sprinkle on pine nuts and pat lightly into dough. Bake in 350°F oven for 20 to 25 minutes or until shortbread is golden. Cool in pans on wire racks for 10 minutes. While still warm, cut into 12 equal wedges. Store wedges in airtight container at room temperature for up to two weeks.

Ginger-spice Waffles

1 c. all-purpose flour
1 c. whole-wheat flour
2 tbsp. unsweetened cocoa powder
1 tbsp. ground ginger
1½ tsp. baking soda
1½ tsp. ground cinnamon
1 tsp. ground nutmeg
½ tsp. salt
2 eggs

1¾ c. buttermilk
¾ c. (1½ sticks) butter or
    margarine, melted
⅓ c. molasses
1½ c. low-fat vanilla yogurt
3 c. fruit, such as blueberries,
    chopped kiwi, and
    mandarin oranges

Sift together all-purpose flour, whole-wheat flour, cocoa powder, ginger, baking soda, cinnamon, nutmeg, and salt into large bowl. Beat eggs slightly in medium-sized bowl. Beat in buttermilk and melted butter until well blended. Make well in center of dry ingredients. Add buttermilk mixture and molasses to well; stir just until ingredients are combined and dry ingredients are moistened. Make 6 waffles in waffle maker following manufacturer's directions. Stack between sheets of waxed paper on large baking sheet and keep warm in 225°F oven. Serve waffles topped with vanilla yogurt and fruit.

Ginger Muffins and Fruit

1 stick (½ c.) unsalted butter,
    plus more for tins
½ vanilla bean, split
1½ c. flour
½ c. sugar
2½ tsp. baking powder
⅛ tsp. salt
1 tsp. ground ginger

½ tsp. ground cinnamon
½ c. buttermilk
1 large egg
¼ c. roughly chopped
    strawberries (about 3 large
    berries)
¼ c. roughly chopped banana
    (about ½ banana)
½ c. raspberries

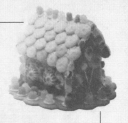

Heat oven to 350°F. Butter 2 minimuffin tins. Scrape seeds from vanilla bean; place pod and seeds into a saucepan. Add butter; place over low heat until melted. Set aside until cooled. Remove and discard pod. Sift flour, sugar, baking powder, salt, ginger, and cinnamon into bowl of an electric mixer. Add reserved melted butter, buttermilk, and egg; mix until just combined. Divide batter in half. Stir strawberries and bananas into half until just combined. Stir raspberries into remaining half of batter. Spoon batter into prepared pans all the way to the top. Bake until golden, 25 to 30 minutes. Remove from oven; set on wire rack until cool.

Vermont Gingerbread Muffins

½ c. melted shortening
½ c. sugar
½ c. molasses
½ c. sour milk (If you don't have
    sour milk, add 2 tsp. vinegar
    to ½ c. milk.)

½ c. sweet milk
2 tsp. baking soda
3 tsp. ginger
1 tsp. cinnamon
2 c. flour
2 eggs

Mix sugar, baking soda, ginger, cinnamon, and flour. Add shortening, molasses, then both milks. Beat in eggs one at a time. Grease muffin tins and fill ⅔ full. Bake at 350°F for 20 to 25 minutes.

old-fashioned griddlecakes

2 c. yellow cornmeal
1 c. flour
1 tsp. salt
pinch of powdered ginger
½ tsp. powdered cinnamon
2 c. sour milk

1 tbsp. molasses
1 tsp. soda
½ c. powdered sugar
¼ lb. butter
2 tsp. cinnamon

Sift together cornmeal, flour, salt, ginger, and cinnamon. Gradually stir in enough sour milk to make a stiff batter. Dissolve a generous table-spoon of molasses in a little hot water, add a level teaspoon of soda, and stir until the mixture foams up. Stir this mixture into the batter and bake

on a hot buttered griddle as for pancakes. Use a tablespoon to drop them onto the griddle in an oval shape rather than round, without making them too large. Allow cakes to get nicely brown and crispy before turning to brown the other side. They should be about ½-inch thick when baked.

Cream ¼ lb. (1 stick) butter with ½ c. powdered sugar and 2 tsp. cinnamon. Serve over top of griddlecakes.

Easy Gingerbread Pancakes

1 tbsp. each ground cinnamon and ginger
4 c. buttermilk pancake mix, complete
2⅓ c. water mixed with ½ c. molasses

Stir spices into pancake mix, then add the molasses mixture just until moistened. Heat lightly oiled griddle or large nonstick skillet over medium heat. Pour pancakes on griddle and cook 4 to 5 minutes, turning once, until puffed and lightly browned. Serve with chunky cinnamon applesauce or Maple Whipped Cream.

MAPLE WHIPPED CREAM:
1½ c. heavy (whipping) cream   ½ c. maple-flavored pancake syrup

Beat cream and syrup until soft peaks form when beaters are lifted. Refrigerate up to 2 hours before serving. If mixture separates, whisk to blend.

gingerbread pudding

½ c. sugar
½ c. molasses
1 c. boiling water
½ c. butter

1 tsp. soda
1 tsp. cinnamon
1 tsp. ginger
flour

Fill a 2-quart baking dish half full of quartered apples. Sprinkle a mixture containing ½ c. sugar, 1 tsp. cinnamon, ¼ tsp. nutmeg, and a pinch of salt over top, then pour ½ c. water over all. Make the gingerbread from the above ingredients using enough flour to make a thick batter; spread over apples and bake at 350°F for 30 minutes.

ginger coconut cake

⅔ c. molasses
½ c. sugar
½ c. butter or other shortening
1 tsp. ginger
1 tsp. cinnamon

1 tsp. baking soda
2 c. sifted cake flour
1 c. sour milk
2 eggs, beaten

Heat first 5 ingredients to boiling, stirring constantly. Cool to lukewarm. Sift soda and flour together and add alternately with milk and eggs, beating thoroughly. Pour into greased muffin pans. Bake in a 350°F oven 15 minutes. Cover with boiled frosting and coconut.

Fig and Ginger Pudding

½ lb. crystallized ginger   ½ tsp. powdered ginger
1½ lbs. figs   ½ oz. (1 tbsp.) granulated gelatin
2 c. sugar   ½ c. cold water
5 c. water   whipped cream

Cut the crystallized ginger and figs into tiny pieces. Dissolve the granulated sugar in the water and add the powdered ginger, the crystallized ginger, and the figs. Place all in a double boiler and simmer slowly all day. The entire mass must form a soft pulp so that the ingredients will scarcely be recognized. Soften the gelatin in the cold water and stir into the mixture while hot. Turn into high-stemmed glasses and serve ice cold with whipped cream.

Gingerbread-Raisin Scones

2 c. all-purpose flour
⅓ c. packed dark brown sugar
1 tbsp. baking powder
¾ tsp. ground cinnamon
½ tsp. ground ginger
6 tbsp. (¾ stick) chilled butter,
  cut into pieces

¼ c. milk
1 large egg
3 tbsp. light molasses
1 tsp. vanilla extract
⅔ c. raisins
⅛ tsp. ground cloves

Preheat oven to 375°F. Lightly grease baking sheet. Blend first 6 ingredients in processor. Add butter and process until mixture resembles coarse meal. Beat milk, egg, molasses, and vanilla and blend in large bowl. Add flour mixture and raisins; stir gently until dough forms. Gather dough into ball. On lightly floured surface, press dough into 1-inch-thick round. Cut round into 8 wedges. Place on prepared baking sheet. Bake until toothpick inserted into center comes out clean, about 25 minutes. Serve warm.

sweetheart ginger scones

2 c. all-purpose flour
2 tsp. baking powder
½ tsp. salt
¼ c. cold butter, cut into pieces

3 tbsp. each sugar and
  minced crystallized ginger
⅔ c. plus 1 tbsp. milk, divided
⅓ c. red currant preserves

Preheat oven to 425°F. In bowl, combine first flour, baking powder, and salt. Using fork, cut in butter to make fine crumbs. Stir in sugar, ginger, and ⅔ c. milk until dough comes together. On floured surface, knead 5–6 times; roll out to ¾-inch thickness. Using 4-inch biscuit cutter, cut out six shapes, rerolling scraps if necessary. Brush with remaining 1 tbsp. milk and bake on lightly greased baking sheet 8–10 minutes or until golden. Cool on wire racks, then split. Evenly spread preserves among scones.

Gingerscotch Cake

Prepare 1 package 2-layer-size butterscotch cake mix using package directions. Stir in ½ cup chopped walnuts, 2 tablespoons chopped candied ginger, and one 1-ounce square semisweet chocolate, grated. Bake in 2 greased and lightly floured 8 x 1½-inch round pans at 350°F for 35 minutes. Cool 10 minutes; remove from pan.

Ginger Sundae Sauce

In small saucepan, mix ⅓ cup light corn syrup, ¼ cup finely chopped candied ginger, dash salt, and ¼ cup light cream. Simmer 5 minutes. Gradually stir in ¼ cup light cream. Heat through, but do not boil. Remove from heat; stir in ¼ cup butter and ½ tsp. vanilla. Serve warm over vanilla ice cream.

Ginger Fruit Freeze

Mix one 3-ounce package cream cheese, softened, 3 tablespoons mayonnaise, 1 tablespoon lemon juice, and ¼ teaspoon salt.

Stir in ½ cup chopped preserved kumquats, ½ cup dates, cut up, ¼ cup quartered maraschino cherries, one 8¾-ounce can crushed pineapple, drained, and 2 tablespoons finely chopped candied ginger.

Fold in 1 cup whipping cream, whipped. Pour into 1-quart refrigerator tray. Sprinkle ½ cup toasted slivered almonds over top. Freeze firm. Makes 6 to 8 servings.

Gingersnap Crust

A good piecrust for almost any fruit-filled pie.

Mix 1½ cups fine gingersnap crumbs and ¼ cup softened butter or margarine. Press firmly into buttered 9-inch pie plate. Bake at 375°F about 9 minutes. Cool. Fill with pie filling of your choice.

Ginger Sherbet

2 qts. water
3 c. sugar
6 lemons
1 tbsp. gelatin

¼ c. syrup from Canton ginger
1 tsp. powdered ginger
2 egg whites

Boil water and sugar together for 5 minutes. Add lemon juice, gelatin softened in a little cold water, the syrup, and the powdered ginger. Freeze to a mush, then stir in the beaten egg whites. Serve in sherbet glasses.

Ginger-Pumpkin Chiffon Pie

1 package (3 oz.) cream cheese, softened

1 tbsp. sugar

1 carton (4 oz.) frozen whipped topping, thawed (1½ cups)

1 graham cracker crust (8 or 9 inches)

1 c. cold milk

2 packages (3.4 oz. each) instant vanilla pudding mix

1 can (16 oz.) pumpkin

1 tsp. ground cinnamon

½ tsp. ground ginger

¼ tsp. ground cloves

OPTIONAL:

chopped nuts and/or additional whipped topping

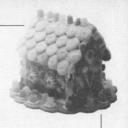

In a mixing bowl, beat cream cheese and sugar until smooth. Add whipped topping and mix well. Spread into crust. In another bowl, beat milk and pudding mixes on low speed until combined; beat on high for 2 minutes. Let stand 3 minutes. Stir in pumpkin and spices; mix well. Spread over cream cheese layer. Chill. Garnish with nuts and/or whipped topping if desired.

coffee ginger cake

2⅓ c. cake flour
1 tsp. soda
1 tsp. ginger
½ tsp. cloves
½ tsp. allspice
1½ tsp. cinnamon

1 tsp. salt
1 c. butter
1¼ c. brown sugar
2 eggs beaten
⅔ c. cold strong coffee

Sift dry ingredients together 3 times. Cream butter and sugar until fluffy. Add eggs and beat well. Add flour alternately with coffee, beating after each addition. Turn into 2 greased 9-inch layer pans. Bake 25 minutes at 375°F.

Ginger~Applesauce Bars

Heat oven to 350°F. Make batter as directed for gingerbread mix—except reduce water to ¼ cup; mix 1 cup applesauce, ½ cup raisins, and ½ cup finely chopped nuts into batter. Spread in greased and floured jelly roll pan, 15½ x 10½ x 1 inches. Bake 12 to 15 minutes. Frost with butter icing.

Orange Nut Ginger Bars

Heat oven to 350°F. Make batter as directed on gingerbread mix package—except reduce water to ½ cup; fold in 1 tablespoon grated orange rind (1 orange) and 1 cup chopped nuts. Pour into 2 greased square pans, each 9 x 9 x 1¾ inches. Bake 12 to 15 minutes. While still warm, frost with orange-flavored icing.

6

Other Gingery Dishes

Dost thou think, because thou art virtuous,
there shall be no more cakes? . . . .
Yes, and ginger shall be hot i' the mouth too.
WILLIAM SHAKESPEARE

Cakes, cookies, and other desserts aren't the only way to use ginger. It's also a tasty ingredient in other dishes, as the recipes that follow demonstrate so well.

Ginger Beef

3 tbsp. oil
1 lb. beef steak

1/3 c. thinly sliced ginger
2 tbsp. oyster sauce

Measure oil. Slice steak into pieces 2 inches long by 1 inch wide by 1/4-inch thick. Measure ginger and oyster sauce. Set by the stove in order listed. Set wok over high heat for 30 seconds; swirl in oil; heat to almost smoking; add beef and stir-fry 1 minute. Add ginger, and stir-fry 4 minutes. Add oyster sauce and stir-fry 2 minutes more. Serve at once.

Ginger Dip

½ c. mayonnaise
½ c. dairy sour cream
1 tbsp. finely chopped onion
2 tbsp. snipped parsley
2 tbsp. finely chopped canned
    water chestnuts

1 tbsp. finely chopped
    candied ginger
1 clove garlic, minced
1½ tsp. soy sauce

Combine mayonnaise and sour cream. Stir in remaining ingredients; chill. Spread over crackers or use as chip dip.

soy Ginger Marinade

This marinade goes well with fish.

¼ c. soy sauce
¼ c. water
¼ c. lemon juice

1 tsp. minced garlic
1 tbsp. minced fresh
    ginger

steamed spinach and ginger

3 tbsp. oil
1 finely chopped shallot
   or mild onion
2 crushed garlic cloves

1 tbsp. grated fresh ginger
1½ lbs. spinach
salt to taste

Warm the oil and simmer the onion, garlic, and ginger until soft. Raise the heat and add the spinach. Cook fast for 1 minute, stirring constantly. Add a pinch of salt, cover the pan, and steam for a few more minutes until tender.

Gingered Rhubarb Jam

4 c. diced fresh rhubarb
3 c. sugar
3 tbsp. finely snipped candied ginger

2 tbsp. lemon juice
a few drops red food coloring

Combine rhubarb with next 3 ingredients in large saucepan; let stand about 15 minutes, or till sugar is moistened by juice. Cook over medium-high heat, stirring frequently till thick and clear, 12 to 15 minutes. Skim off foam; add red food coloring, if desired. Ladle into hot sterilized jars; seal. Makes 3 half-pints.

Ginger Punch

1 qt. water
1 c. sugar
¾ c. chopped Canton
    ginger

¼ c. ginger syrup
1 c. orange juice
¼ c. lemon juice
1 qt. seltzer water

Boil water, sugar, ginger, and ginger syrup for 20 minutes. Cool. Add fruit juices and seltzer water gradually.

7
ginger crafts

Enough if something from our hands have power
To live, and act, and serve the future hour.
WILLIAM WORDSWORTH

There's something very satisfying about making something with our hands, especially at Christmastime. These gingery crafts leave a lasting memory of the season—or many of them can be enjoyed with the eyes for a while and then eventually eaten. These crafts add a festive air to your holiday celebrations, and many of them make wonderful gifts, as well. What a homey and spicy way to show Christ's love this Christmas!

gingerbread-cookie ornaments
(edible, too)

¼ lb. (1 stick) margarine,
    at room temperature
½ c. loosely packed dark brown sugar
½ c. molasses
3½ c. sifted all-purpose flour
1 tsp. baking soda

1 tsp. ground cinnamon
1 tsp. ground ginger
½ tsp. salt
¼ tsp. ground cloves
Royal Icing (recipe follows)
silver balls for decorating

Cream together the margarine and sugar. Add the molasses and mix well. Sift together dry ingredients. With mixer on low speed, slowly add dry ingredients and ⅓ c. water to molasses mixture. If dough gets too stiff, mix with your hands. Work dough with your hands until smooth.

Turn out onto a piece of plastic wrap, form into a neat rectangle, wrap well, and refrigerate for at least 1 hour or overnight.

Roll out dough to just under ¼-inch thick. Cut out as many cookies as possible. Heat oven to 350°F. Place cookies on parchment-lined baking sheets and bake for 10 to 15 minutes, or until firm. When the cookies are just out of the oven, use a bamboo or metal skewer to make a small hole ½ inch from the top of each one to accommodate a hook or cord. After cookies cool, spread a layer of icing on each one and decorate as desired with silver balls in assorted sizes. Reinsert skewers to keep holes open. To allow icing to set, leave cookies for 30 minutes in an oven on the lowest setting.

ROYAL ICING:
2 large egg whites
4 c. sifted confectioners' sugar
juice of 1 lemon

3 drops glycerine
(available at pharmacies)

Beat the egg whites until stiff but not dry. Add sugar, lemon juice, and glycerine, and beat for 1 minute more. If icing is too thick, add a little water. If too thin, add more sugar.

Easy Gingerbread House

For the feeling of a gingerbread house without the complex construction, make a one-dimensional façade. Trace a large pattern for your "house" on cardboard. Use this cardboard pattern on rolled out cookie dough; cut out house and bake. After cooling, pipe white Royal Icing to create details such as windows, roof, doors, and more. Prop on a fireplace mantel and surround with evergreens and berries.

Gingerbread Wreath

Make Ginger Crisps (p. 28) dough; roll it out onto a well-floured work surface. Cut about 60 leaf shapes from the dough (use a couple of different cutters), and place the leaves on a parchment-lined baking sheet. Refrigerate until chilled, about 20 minutes. Using the back of a paring knife, press "vein" patterns into each leaf. Line another baking sheet with parchment. Using a dinner plate or cake pan as a template, draw an 8- or 9-inch circle on the paper. Place the leaves around the circle, brushing a bit of water with a pastry brush onto the back of each leaf

before placing it over the next one. Overlap and stagger the leaves in the form of a wreath. Chill the wreath, about 20 minutes. Heat the oven to 350°F, and bake the wreath until crisp but not darkened, 12 to 15 minutes. Transfer wreath to a wire rack, and let cool overnight. To decorate, stand wreath against your arm at an angle, and sprinkle with confectioners' sugar put through a sieve; better yet, have someone use both hands to hold the wreath at an angle while you work. Ideally, the sugar on top of the gingerbread leaves will look like snowfall on real leaves. Attach a bow and hang away from heat or moisture.

gingerbread gift container

The container can be made in any shape; for example a 6-sided container would be made with 8 pieces, 1 piece for the top, 1 for the bottom, and 6 for the sides. Cut out the shapes you want in cardboard, and then use them to trace shapes in the gingerbread dough. Make a small hole in the center of the top piece. Bake, cool, and then glue the pieces together with Royal Icing, which dries very hard; the seams are then covered with decorative dots of icing. To make a handle, put a ribbon through the hole in the top, and tie a knot on the underside. Fill with cookies, candies, or any other small gift you wish.

Gingerbread Button Cookies

Prepare dough for gingerbread and cut out round shapes with a cookie cutter. Add an inner ring by gently pressing the rim of a glass into the dough. Poke 4 button holes into each cookie with a skewer, and bake. Stack several cooled cookies, and thread a thin ribbon through the holes. Line gingerbread container (p.135) with tissue paper, and arrange cookies inside. Tie a ribbon around outside of container and sew a ribbon through some buttons (real ones) for added effect.

gingerbread garland

MATERIALS

gingerbread men pattern (Trace
    around a cookie cutter if you
    don't want to draw one yourself.)

tracing paper

pencil

chalk pencil

two 8 x 10-inch pieces of tan felt

white baby rickrack

Tacky (white) glue

$\frac{1}{8}$-inch satin ribbon—
    $1\frac{2}{3}$ yards of red and
    $\frac{2}{3}$ yard of green

8 $\frac{1}{8}$-inch black beads

12 cranberry pony beads

scissors

red acrylic paint

fine paintbrush

See instructions on next two pages.

CUTOUTS:
Trace pattern onto tracing paper and cut out pattern. Cut out gingerbread men. Forming the fronts, on 4 of the cutouts, glue rickrack to arms and legs and add black beads for eyes. Also paint a smile on each face. Let dry.

Cut two 4-inch pieces of both red and green ribbon. Tie each into a bow. Glue to the necks of the front pieces. Glue a red heart to the front of each. Let dry.

GARLAND:

Cut four 12-inch pieces of red ribbon. Cut three 4-inch pieces of green ribbon. Thread 4 pony beads onto each green ribbon piece.

Position the remaining cutouts (backs) 3 inches apart on a flat surface. Glue a piece of green ribbon with pony beads between cutouts. Glue 2 pieces of red ribbon extending out from each end of garland.

Add a bead of glue around outer edge of each back piece and glue a front right side up to each back, alternating red and green.

Tie garland onto tree with red ribbons.

cinnamon stick wallhanging

Make this primitive frame cleverly constructed from left-over cinnamon sticks. Fuse and embroider a simple design on muslin featuring your favorite gingerbread recipe, and you'll have a charming new addition to your holiday decorations.

MATERIALS

four large, ¾-inch cinnamon sticks, 12-inch lengths

jute twine

fabrics: unbleached muslin, 9 x 12 inches; golden brown brushed denim, 4-inch square; 3 coordinating small prints, 2-inch squares

fusible web

fine-line black permanent marking pen

embroidery floss: green; tan

four ¾-inch, flat dark red buttons
quilt batting, 9 x 14 inches
miscellaneous items: tracing paper; pencil; ruler; scissors;
    lightweight cardboard, 9 x 14 inches; embroidery
    needle; masking tape; iron; craft wire; wirecutters; hot glue gun

To make the frame, cut 2 cinnamon sticks to 9-inches. Position the 12-inch sticks on top of the shorter sticks at right angles, creating an approximately 6½ x 8½-inch frame opening. Tie the sticks together at the corners with the jute twine, knotting the twine at the back. Spot glue the sticks on the back to secure.

Refer to the manufacturer's instructions to fuse the web to the wrong side of the brushed denim and print fabrics. Trace your own small, simple patterns for a heart, star, and gingerbread man and cut them out. Center the traced recipe under the muslin and use the marking pen to trace the recipe onto the muslin.

Fuse the gingerbread man, hearts, and the star onto the muslin. Use the marking pen to draw the eyes on the gingerbread man and "stitching lines" around each appliqué.

Sew the buttons to the muslin with tan embroidery floss. Backstitch "stems" with green floss, emanating from the buttons. Also, use the tan floss to embroider three X's for buttons down the center front of the gingerbread man.

To assemble the picture, cut the quilt batting and the lightweight cardboard each into two 7 x 9-inch pieces. Layer the muslin, right side down, with both batting pieces and one cardboard rectangle on top. Pull the edges of the muslin onto the back of the cardboard, stretching the design taut, and tape to secure. Center and glue the remaining cardboard rectangle over the taped back. Place the design in the frame from the back and spot glue along the edges to secure. To hang, cut a length of craft wire to fit, and thread the ends through the jute at the top back corners of the design. Twist the wire ends to secure.

Felt Gingerbread Man Ornament

MATERIALS

9 x 12 inch square brown felt

shiny white plaid fashion fabric paint

½ yard each of ⅜-inch red polka-dot grosgrain and
   ⅛-inch green satin ribbons

polyester fiberfill

red or green embroidery floss

embroidery needle

pinking shears

tracing paper

air-soluble fabric marker

dressmaker's white carbon paper or other transfer paper

See instructions on next page.

Cut felt in half into 6 x 9-inch blocks. Trace gingerbread man pattern. Transfer outline (seam line) with marker to center of one block; transfer major clothing lines with carbon.

Paint designs (not seam line), starting at top and practice using paint first. Let dry.

Pin blocks together right side out. Thread needle with floss; knot end. Hiding knot between layers, sew running stitches along seam line; stuff from side before completing round.

Trim edges with pinking shears.

Glue or tack ends of 2-inch red ribbon to top back for loop. Tie bow of red and green ribbons held together; tack or glue to top front.

gingerbread cookie bag

MATERIALS

⅓ yard unbleached muslin

¾ yard calico fabric (During the holidays, you can often find calico
   prints featuring gingerbread men.)

6-inch by 25-inch piece of fusible fabric

1 yard of ½-inch grosgrain ribbon

gingerbread cookie cutter

wooden spoon

your favorite recipe for gingerbread cookies and dry ingredients

pinking shears

rubber band

Note: Do not include sugar with the dry ingredients.

Cut two 10-inch by 13-inch pieces of muslin.

Cut two 10-inch-long pieces of the border print. Pink edges of border print (top and bottom).

Iron fusible fabric onto backs of border pieces. Iron border pieces onto muslin, 1½ inches up from bottom.

With right sides together, stitch the seam allowance around 2 sides and bottom of muslin pieces. Turn right side out and pink top edges.

Fill bag with dry ingredients using desired recipe. Close top of sack tightly with rubber band. Tie ribbon around rubber band. Slide wooden spoon behind ribbon or rubber band.

Write recipe for gingerbread cookies on recipe card. Stamp card with gingerbread rubber stamps. Punch hole in corner using hole punch. Attach card to ribbon. Tie on cookie cutter.

gingerbread cookie wreath

This one is different from the one a few pages earlier; this one is edible and playful looking, not elegant looking like the other. Serve this wreath at a caroling party or any occasion—it's a holiday decoration that's good enough to eat. It makes a fun centerpiece at a luncheon or a children's party.

1 package (14½ oz.) gingerbread cake/cookie mix or 2 cups gingerbread
    cookie dough of your choice
musical note cookie cutter (4 inches)
holly leaf cookie cutter (1½ inches)
½ lb. white confectionery coating*, melted
¼ c. green colored sugar
pastry bag or small heavy-duty resealable plastic bag
pastry tip (#3 round)
15 cinnamon candies

Prepare mix according to package directions for cookies. Set aside ¼ cup dough. On a greased baking sheet, roll out remaining dough into a 9½-inch circle. With a sharp knife, cut a 4-inch circle from the center of the 9½-inch circle. Remove 4-inch circle; add to reserved dough. Bake 9½-inch ring at 375°F for 12–15 minutes or until edges are firm (do not over-bake). Cool for 1 minute; remove to a wire rack. Roll out reserved dough to ½-inch thickness. Cut out 5 musical notes and 10 holly leaves. Place 2 inches apart on a greased baking sheet. Bake at 375°F for 10–12 minutes or until edges are firm. Remove to a wire rack to cool. Dip holly leaves

halfway in confectionery coating; sprinkle with green sugar.
Place on ring. Cut a small hole in the corner of pastry or plastic bag; insert round tip. Fill with remaining confectionery coating. Squeeze a small amount on the back of cookies; attach to wreath. Pipe around edges of notes. Pipe small dots of coating above holly leaves to attach candies. Allow coating to set completely, about 30 minutes.

*Confectionery coating is found in the baking section of most grocery stores. It is sometimes labeled "almond bark" or "candy coating" and is often sold in bulk packages of 1 to 1½ pounds.

christmas cookie bowl

This is a tasteful container you can create for your holiday home décor—from gingerbread. Use it as a gift container, a table topper, or, since it is edible, as part of a festive dessert. You can cut out shapes in the sides of your bowl with a cookie cutter and then line the bowl with a bright napkin. The cloth will add color to the outside by showing through the cutouts and keep goodies on the inside. With the dough that's left after you've made the bowl, you can cut out cookies. Or try shaping little containers by forming the dough over custard cups. Once they've baked and cooled, you can fill the cups with nuts or candies.

Make 1 batch of gingerbread according to the following recipe:

½ c. butter or margarine, softened   1 tsp. ground allspice
½ c. sugar   1 tsp. ground ginger
½ c. molasses   1 tsp. ground nutmeg
¼ c. water   ½ tsp. baking soda
2½ c. all-purpose flour

ICING:

6 tbsp. butter or margarine, softened
2⅔ c. confectioners' sugar
1 tsp. vanilla extract

1 to 2 tbsp. milk
food coloring

In a large mixing bowl, cream butter and sugar. Add molasses and water; mix well. Combine flour, allspice, ginger, nutmeg, and baking soda. Add to creamed mixture; mix well. Cover and chill for at least 3 hours.

PREPARING "MOLD":
Spray the outside of $1\frac{1}{2}$-quart ovenproof glass bowl with nonstick cooking spray. Invert bowl and place on ungreased baking sheet.

SHAPING BOWL:
On a floured board, roll out chilled dough into a $\frac{1}{4}$-inch-thick circle. Gently transfer the dough circle to the outside of the bowl. Trim edge of dough 1 inch above bowl rim with a pastry cutter or knife. Cover and refrigerate remaining dough to use for cookies.

If desired, use the 1-inch cookie cutter to cut out shapes around dough bowl. (Be sure to invert the cookie cutter so that when bowl is turned right side up, the shapes will be right side up also.) Chill for 20 minutes.

Bake at 350°F for 20–25 minutes or until edges are lightly browned. Cool gingerbread on bowl. Gently twist bottom of gingerbread bowl until it releases; invert and carefully remove bowl. Place bowl on 9-inch plate or platter. Add candy around bottom of bowl.

MAKING GINGERBREAD COOKIES:

Roll out reserved dough to ½-inch thickness. Cut with 2½-inch cookie cutters. Place cutouts on a greased baking sheet. Bake at 350°F for 10–12 minutes or until edges are lightly brown. Cool completely on a wire rack. Combine icing ingredients. Decorate cookies as desired and serve in bowl.

8

Ginger Facts

Its antiseptic properties and sulfur content made ginger a common antidote for the plague. It stimulates the gastric juices and is warming and soothing for colds and coughs.
SARAH GARLAND

In our world of artificial flavors and factory-produced foods, filled with warnings and worries about foods that may harm us, we often forget that God intended food to be both tasty and healthy. Ginger is a natural substance that comes from a plant—and it's not only tasty; it's good for you, too!

The Ginger Plant

Ginger grows in the rainforests. Although it originated in Southeast Asia, it is now cultivated on a large scale in New Zealand. The island of Jamaica in the British West Indies is our largest supplier.

It is a perennial herb that grows up to a yard tall, bearing fronds of dark green leaves from a thick, underground stem (the ginger rhizome). In the summer, pale yellow, tubular flowers are borne on erect spikes.

The thick root is sometimes known as the "hand," because it can look like a fat hand with strange fingers.

The Ginger Root

The root is the part of the plant used for the spice. When about a year old, the roots are dug up, washed, and dried in the sun. Ginger is available whole and ground. (Crystallized and preserved gingers are considered confections rather than spices.) It is best to buy small amounts of good quality ground ginger, as the volatile essential oil responsible for the flavor is easily lost in the air. Ground ginger should never be substituted in recipes calling for fresh.

Whole ginger root is preferred when making flavored syrups and pickling vinegars. About half an hour of cooking is required to release the flavor. A half-inch of whole ginger lends a delicious aroma to chicken or beef stock. Ground ginger may be used in all baked dishes, or as a last-minute seasoning for soup or sauce.

Medicinal Properties of Ginger

One of the world's oldest and most popular medicinal plants, ginger is used in folk medicine almost everywhere. In China, pungent, tangy ginger tea, made by boiling pieces of fresh ginger in water, has long been used as a remedy for coughs, colds, and flu. The Chinese believe that the tea strengthens the lungs and kidneys. In Japan, a ginger-oil massage is a traditional treatment for spinal and joint problems. Ginger compresses are used in many parts of the world to relieve sinus congestion, kidney problems, menstrual cramps, and various other aches and pains. A piece of cotton soaked in ginger oil is a common treatment for earache. Some herbalists recommend hot ginger compresses and baths to relieve gout, arthritis, headaches, and spinal pain. Candied ginger can be eaten to stimulate appetite. A warm ginger footbath is said to have the effect of invigorating the whole body.

Ginger Therapy

Ginger owes its therapeutic activity mainly to an essential oil that contains, among other substances, camphene, phellandrene, zingiberene, and zingerone. These combine to make ginger effective as an aid to digestion of fatty foods. It also draws blood to the area where it is applied, which accounts for much of its effectiveness in reducing soreness.

ginger joy!

At Christmastime—and all year-round—may the sweet taste of gingerbread add spice to your celebrations. Remember—Christmas is the birthday of our King. Let us celebrate His birth with joy.